Fingerstyle Guitar Tunes

BEAUTIFUL AIRS & BALLADS OF THE BRITISH ISLES

by Raymond Gonzalez

To access the online audio go to:
WWW.MELBAY.COM/30915MEB

The Collings OM2H T image on the cover is courtesy of Collings Guitars.

© 2021 by Mel Bay Publications, Inc. All Rights Reserved.
WWW.MELBAY.COM

Preface

This book offers a collection of lyrical tunes from Ireland, Scotland, Wales and England plus a few original pieces by William Bay. I made every effort to stay as true to the original melodies as possible, keeping intact the intimate and personal qualities that make these songs last through generations. Upon request, the arrangements are in either standard or dropped-D tunings and so accessible to the intermediate player. On occasion, I did take some harmonic and rhythmic liberties which I hope will seem happily unexpected!

I hope you enjoy playing these tunes as much as I did exploring, rethinking and arranging them.

All the best,

Raymond Gonzalez

1. ◊ = natural harmonics
2. If specific fingering is required, it is placed in the manuscript. Otherwise, refer to the tablature for fingering and string placement.

Index

Title	Page	Audio
An Drochshaol (The Hard Times)	4	1
Auld Lang Syne	10	3
Believe Me, if All Those Endearing Young Charms	7	2
Cailin Deas Crúite na mBó (Pretty Girl Milking Her Cow)	12	4
Call the Ewes	15	5
Down by the Sally Gardens	22	7
Fair Flower of Northumberland	24	8
Fields of Culloden	26	9
I Went to Visit the Roses	18	6
Irish Prayer	30	11
Jock O'Hazeldean	32	12
John Anderson, My Jo	36	13
Once I Had a Sweetheart	28	10
Scarborough Fair	38	14
She Moved Through the Fair	40	15
Sí Bheag, Sí Mór	43	16
Star of the County Down	46	17
The Flowers of Sweet Erin the Green	52	19
The Galway Shawl	49	18
The Marsh of Rhuddlan	54	20
The Shearing's Not for You	57	21
The Water Is Wide	60	22
Wild Mountain Thyme	62	23

An Drochshaol
The Hard Times

William Bay
arr. Raymond Gonzalez

Believe Me, if All Those Endearing Young Charms

Thomas Moore
arr. by Raymond Gonzalez

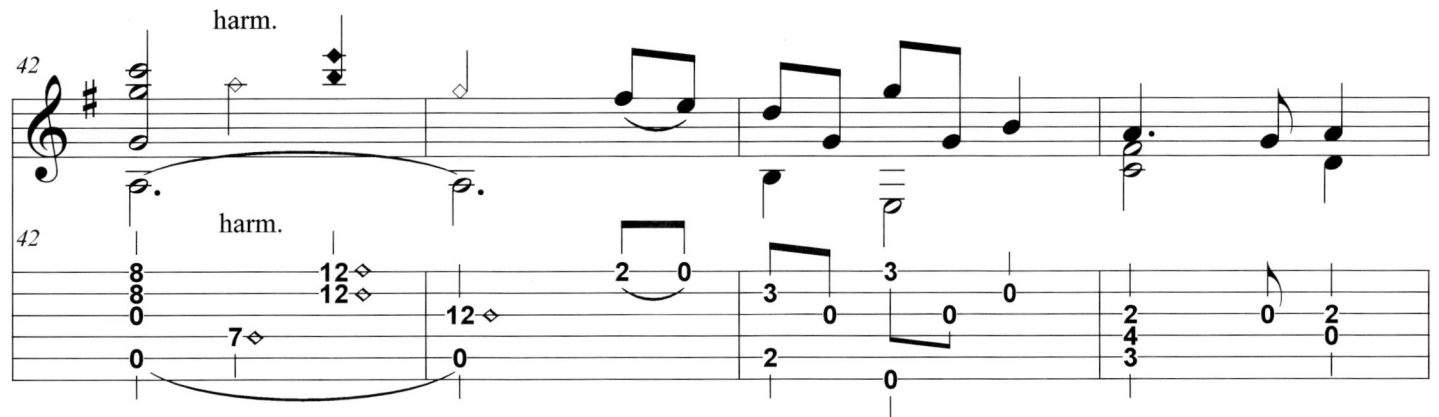

Auld Lang Syne

Robert Burns
arr. by Raymond Gonzalez

© Raymond Gonzalez. All Rights Reserved.

Cailin Deas Crúite na mBó

Pretty Girl Milking Her Cow

arr. by Raymond Gonzalez

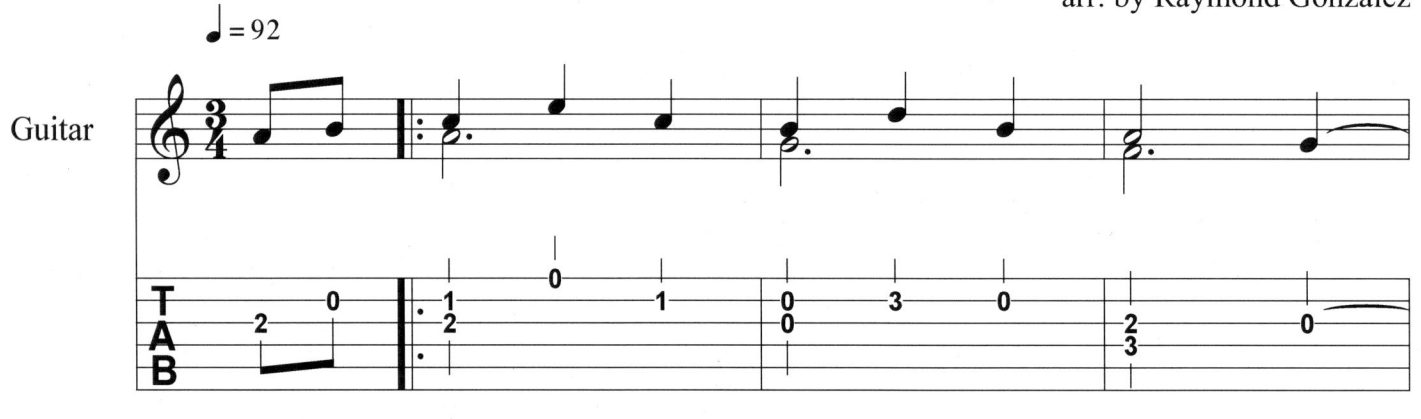
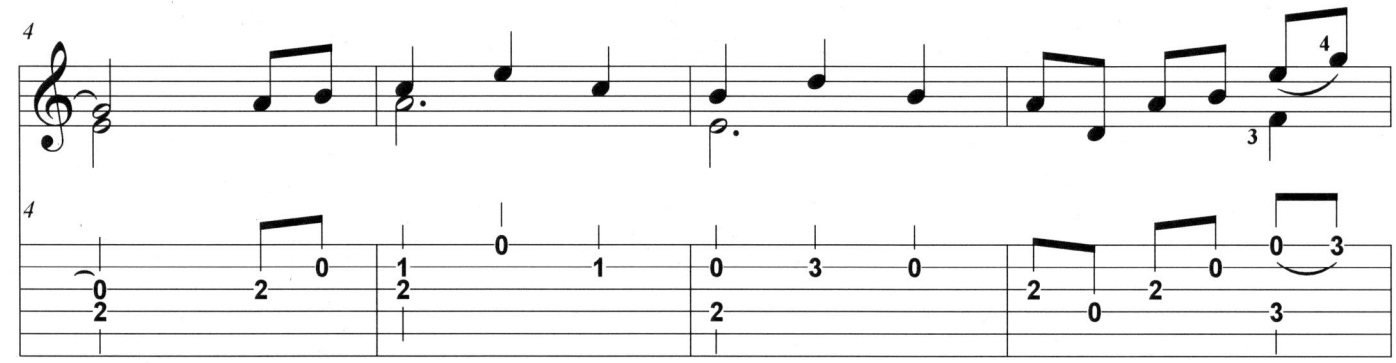

Call the Ewes

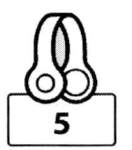

Robert Burns
arr. by Raymond Gonzalez

♩=92

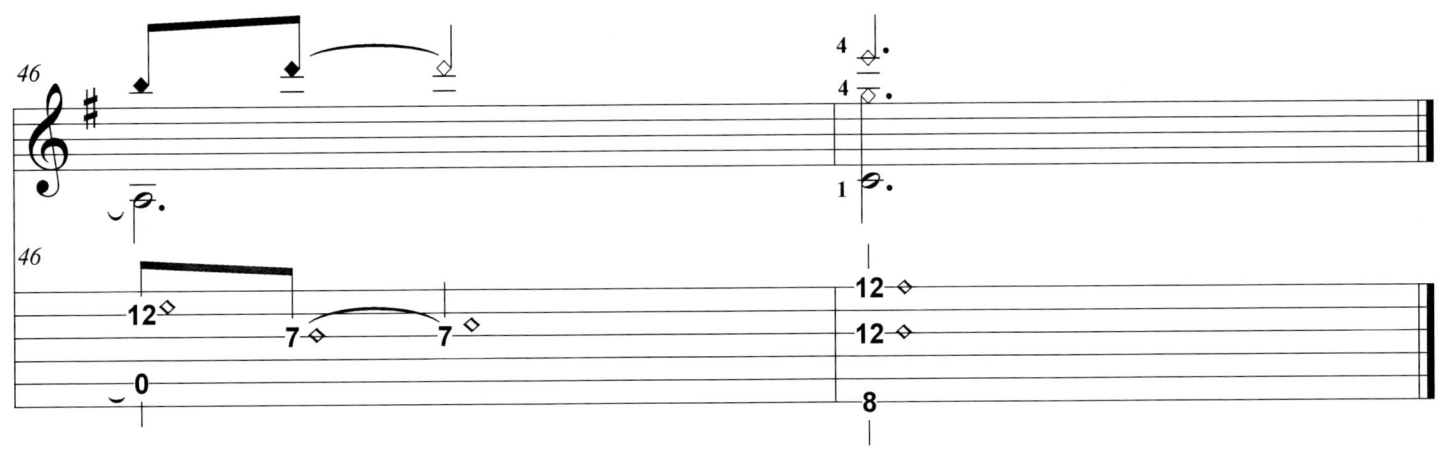

17

I Went To Visit the Roses

arr. by Raymond Gonzalez

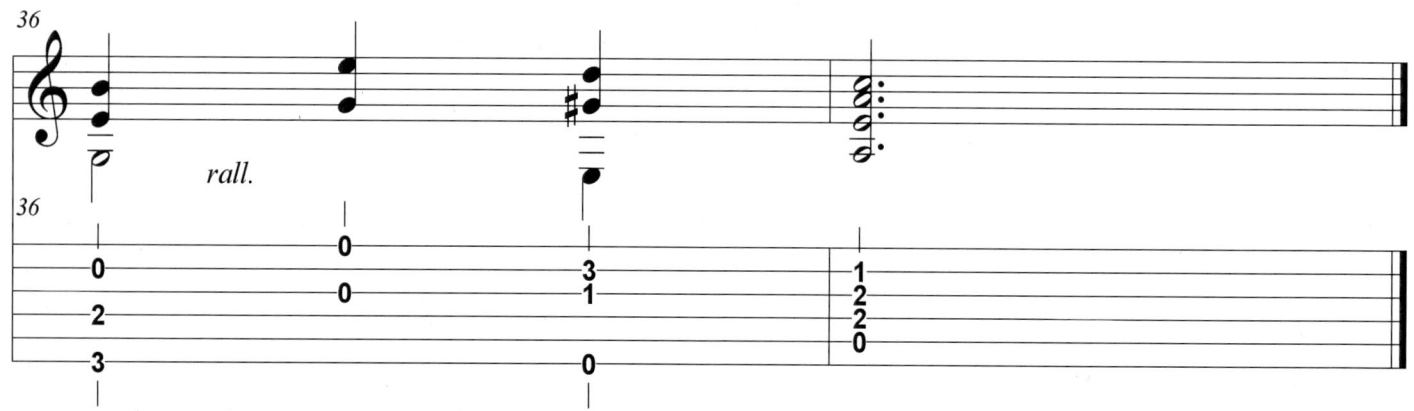

This page has been left blank to avoid an awkward page turn.

Down by the Sally Gardens

Moderate with an easy flow

arr. by Raymond Gonzalez

Fair Flower of Northumberland

Traditional Scottish
arr. by Raymond Gonzalez

Fields of Culloden

William Bay
arr. by Raymond Gonzalez

Once I Had a Sweetheart

arr. by Raymond Gonzalez

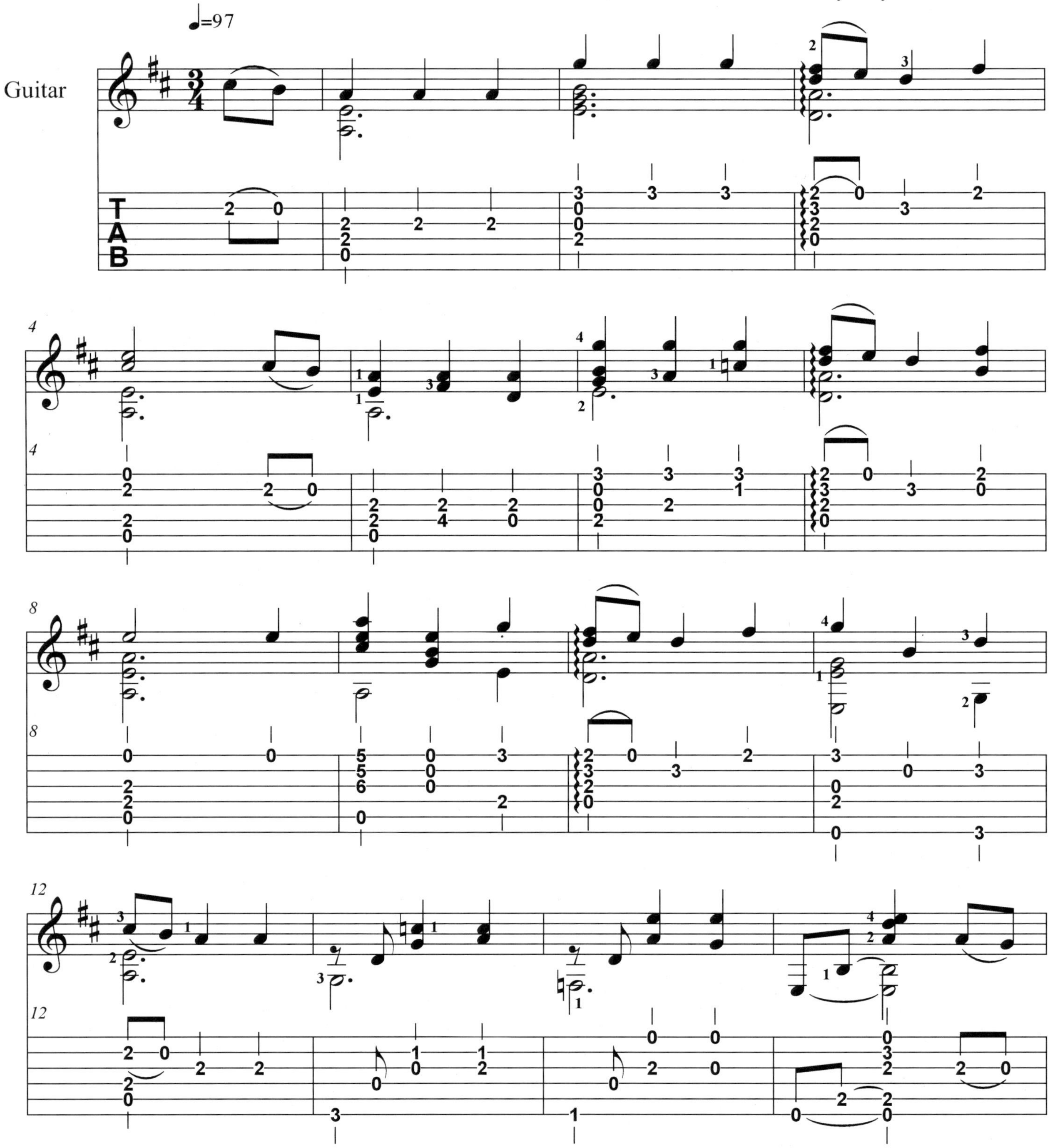

Irish Prayer

William Bay
arr. Raymond Gonzalez

Slow and lyrical

Jock O'Hazeldean

arr. Raymond Gonzalez

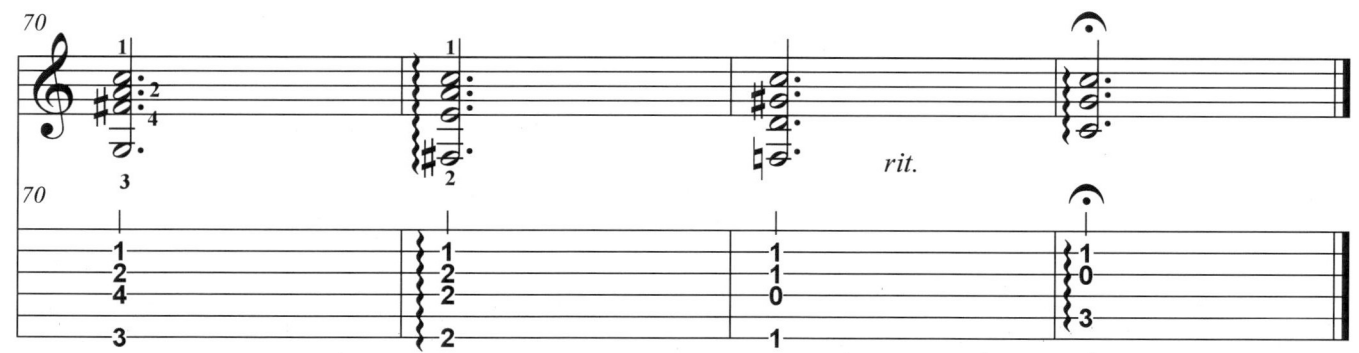

John Anderson, My Jo

arr. Raymond Gonzalez

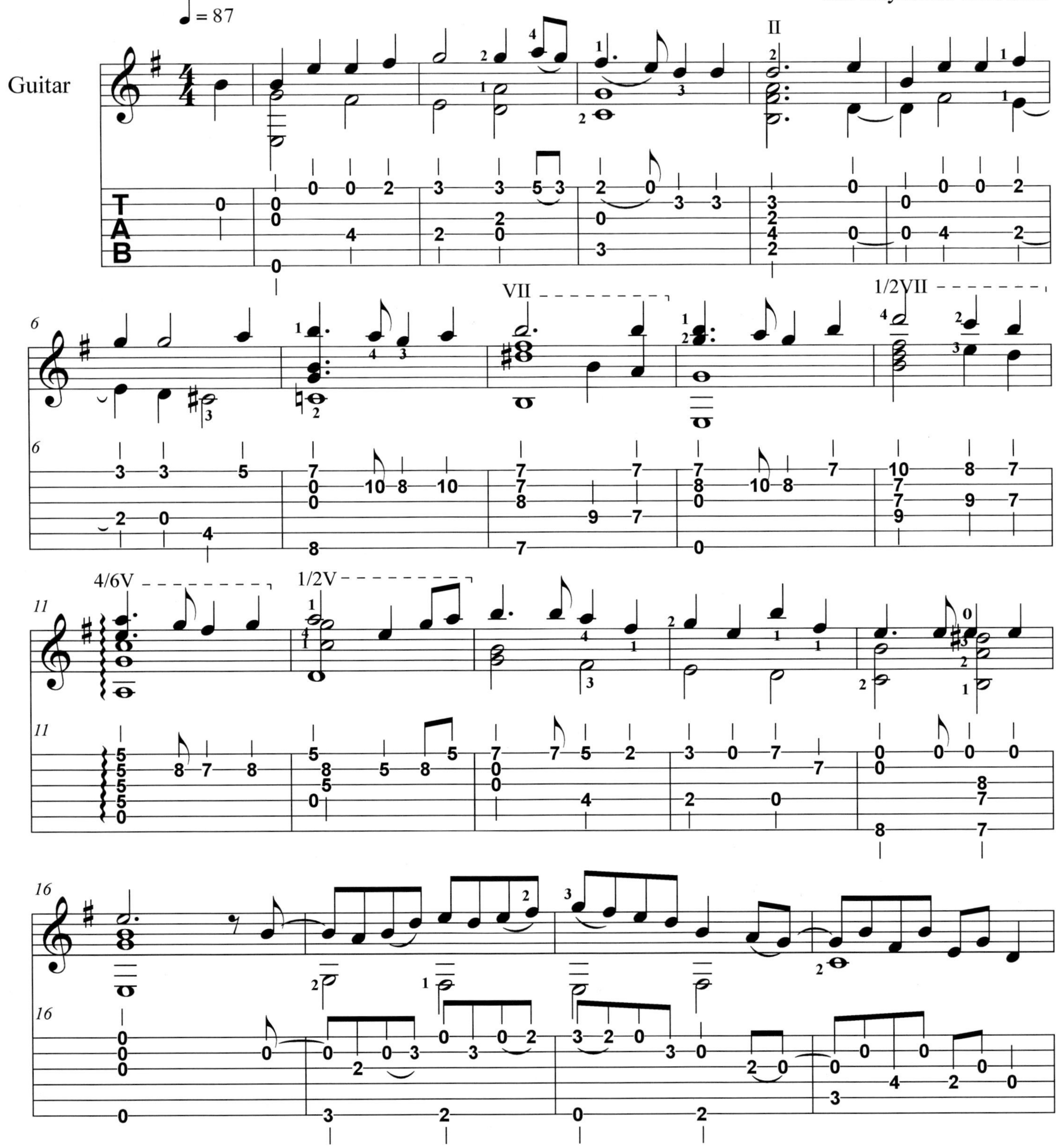

Scarborough Fair

arr. Raymond Gonzalez

She Moved Through the Fair

arr. by Raymond Gonzalez

Sí Bheag, Sí Mór

Turlough O'Carolan
arr. Raymond Gonzalez

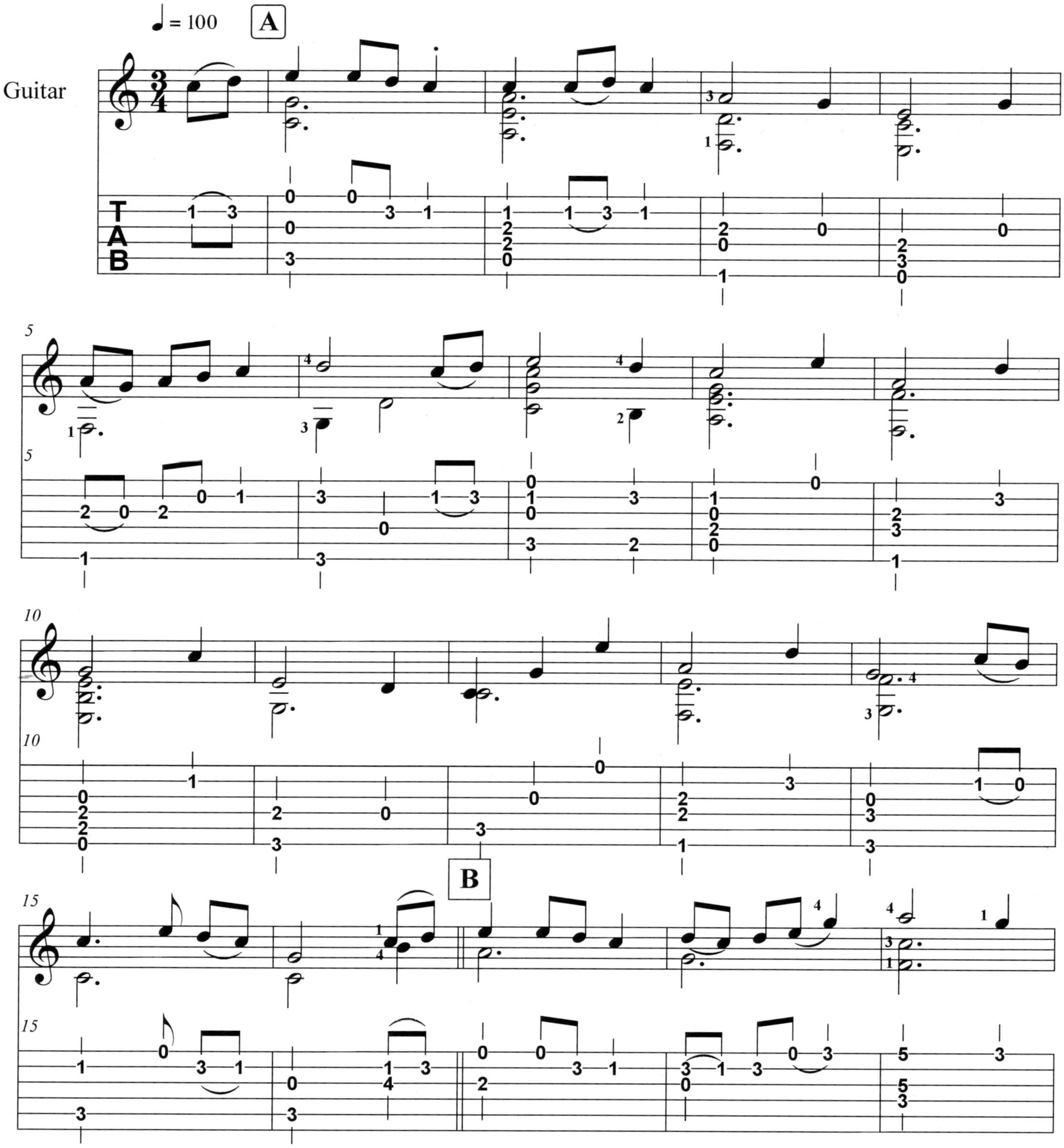

Star of the County Down

arr. Raymond Gonzalez

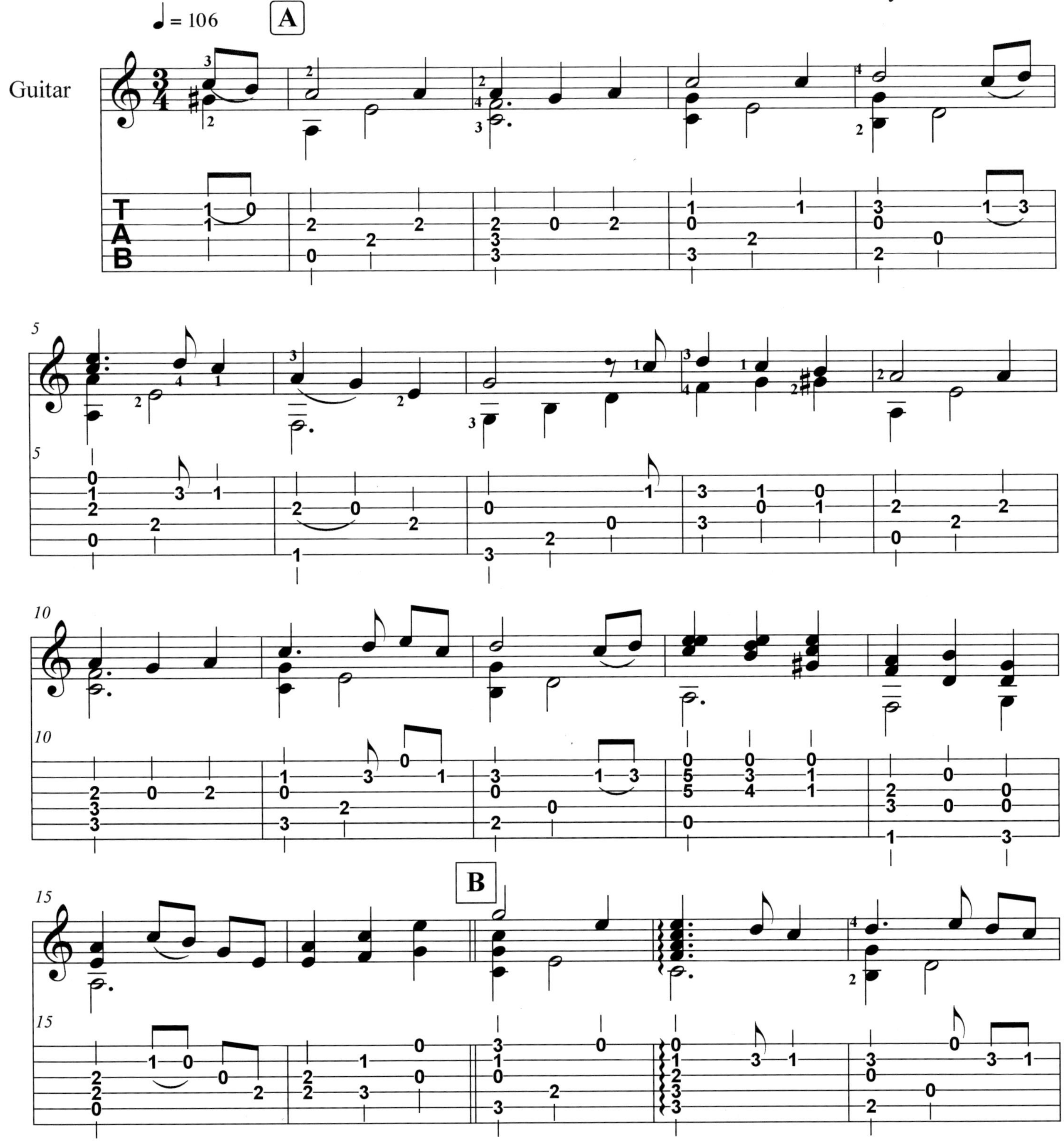

The Galway Shawl

arr. by Raymond Gonzalez

49

The Flowers of Sweet Erin the Green

arr. by Raymond Gonzalez

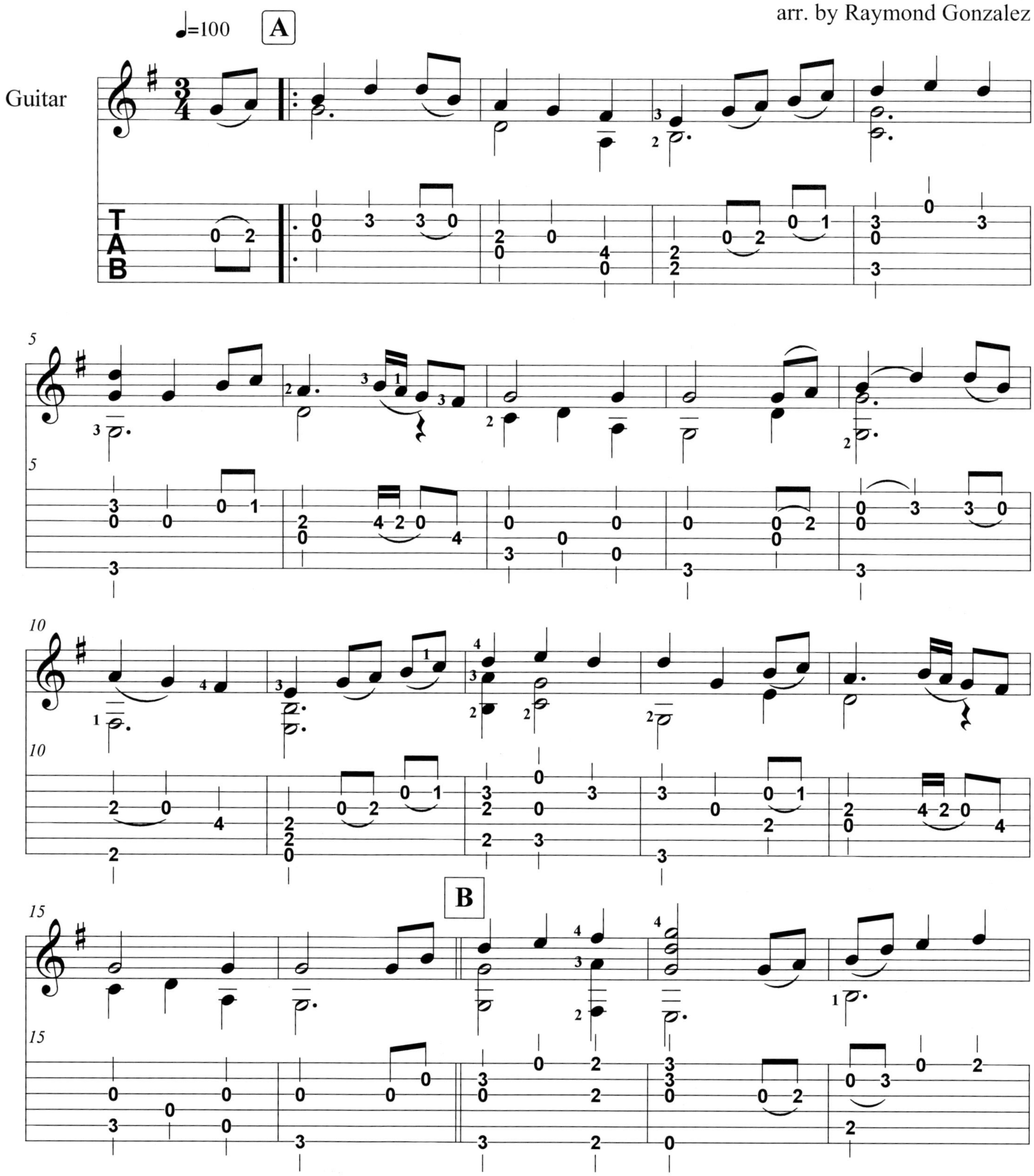

The Marsh of Rhuddlan

arr. by Raymond Gonzalez

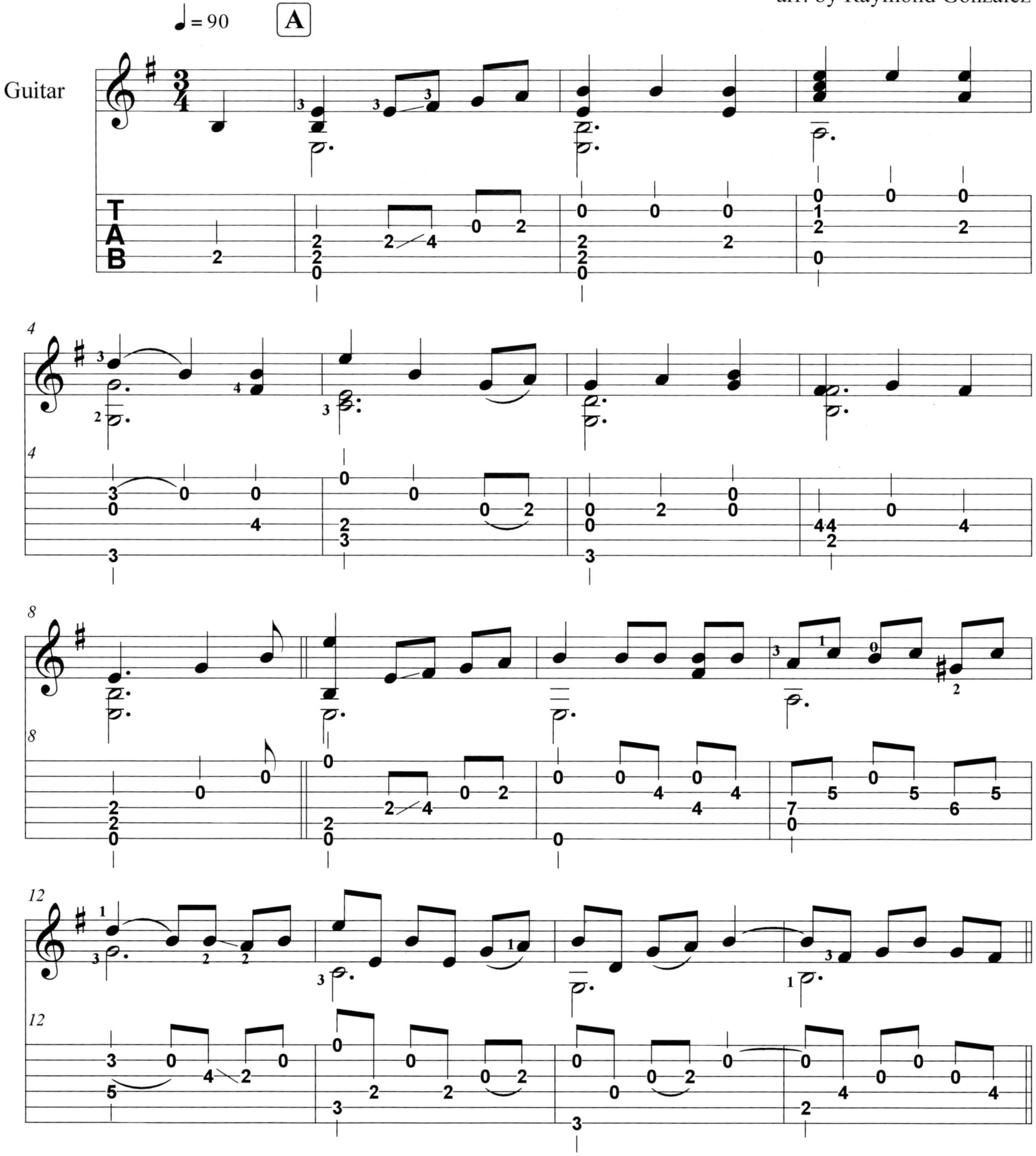

The Shearing's Not for You

arr. Raymond Gonzalez

The Water Is Wide

arr. Raymond Gonzalez

Wild Mountain Thyme

arr. by Raymond Gonzalez

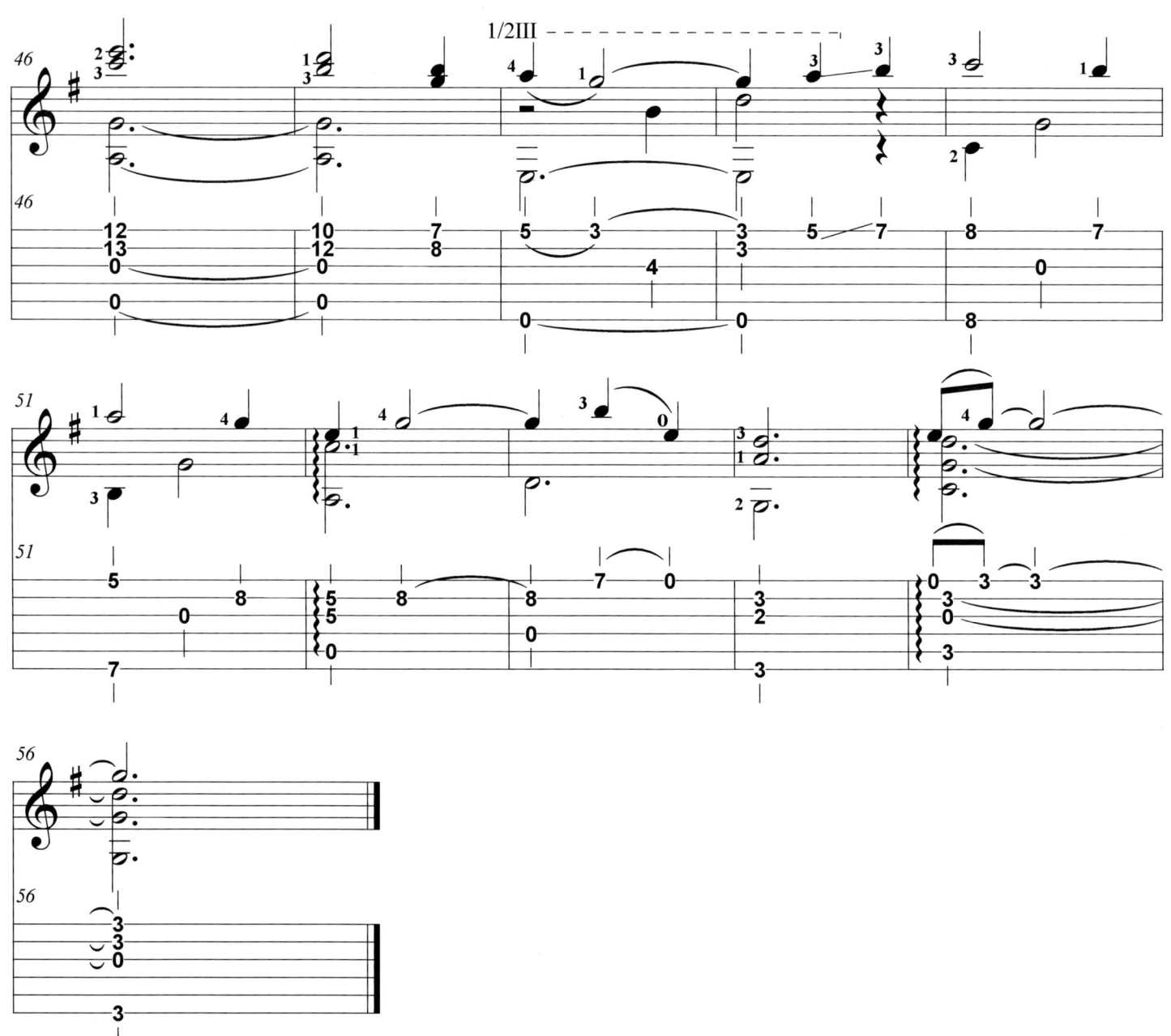